# America's Prairies and Grasslands

## Guide to Plants and Animals

### Marianne D. Wallace

fulcrum resources
Golden, Colorado

Black-tailed Prairie Dog

Deer Mouse

*This book is for those who have already been
to the wonderful world among the grasses, and for those
whose journey has just begun.*

Library of Congress Cataloging-in-Publication Data
Wallace, Marianne D.
  America's  prairies and grasslands : guide to plants and animals / Marianne D. Wallace.
    p. cm.
  ISBN 1-55591-992-8
  1.  Grassland ecology—North America—Juvenile literature. 2.  Prairie ecology—North America—Juvenile literature. 3.  Grasslands—North America—Juvenile literature. 4.  Prairies—North America—Juvenile literature. [1. Grasslands. 2. Prairies. 3. Grassland ecology. 4. Prairie ecology. 5. Ecology.] I. Title.
  QH102 .W35 2001
  577.4'0973—dc21
                                                                        2001001699

Printed in Singapore
0 9 8 7 6 5 4 3 2 1

Fulcrum Publishing
16100 Table Mountain Parkway, Suite 300
Golden, Colorado 80403
(800) 992-2908 • (303) 277-1623
www.fulcrum-resources.com

# TABLE OF CONTENTS

Badger

Burrowing Owl

# Introduction to Prairie and Grassland Life

A **red-tailed hawk** circles slowly above a treeless plain, its keen eyes watching for signs of movement down below. Unaware of any danger, a **thirteen-lined ground squirrel** moves among clumps of grass, hunting for seeds and grasshoppers. The ground squirrel looks up just as the hawk begins its dive. With no place to hide among the grasses, the ground squirrel must

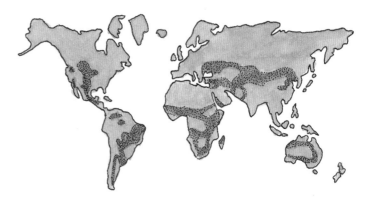

Grasslands cover about ¼ (24%) of the earth's surface.

run as fast as it can to reach the safety of its burrow. The hawk nears, skimming the tops of the grasses, as the ground squirrel finally reaches its burrow hole and jumps in. Cheated of a meal, the hawk settles onto a low dirt mound and waits. It is still early in the day and from its perch it can see far across the open ground, ready to act on any other movement it sees across the plain.

Thirteen-lined Ground Squirrel

There are huge, open areas all over the world where the ground is covered mostly by grasses. These are the "grasslands" and they are found on every continent except Antarctica. They include the pampas of South America, the veld of Africa, the puszta of Europe, the steppe of Asia, the lowlands of Australia, and the prairie of North America. Altogether, grasslands cover more of the earth's surface than any other biome.

Grasslands require three conditions to exist: rain followed by long periods of drought or dry weather, large grazing animals to eat the grasses and other plants, and occasional wildfires. Why are there grasslands? Why aren't these areas eventually covered by trees and shrubs? What types of animals make their homes here?

Grasslands are areas that usually get some winter rain, but are often dry for the rest of the year. Since most grasses grow from spring through summer, they can absorb the water they need while the ground is still moist. By late summer or fall when the ground is dry, the grasses have already flowered and made seeds for the following year. Some grasses remain alive but dormant just beneath the ground, ready to sprout new leaves as soon as the rain and warm weather return the following year. Trees and shrubs often require more water to survive than is available in most of the grassland areas. That's why when you find trees here, they are usually in riparian areas or protected canyons and draws.

But sometimes trees and shrubs get enough water to start growing, sending their long roots into the moist earth that is deep, deep underground. **Deer** and **elk** love to eat the fresh green leaves and young stems of many of these trees and shrubs. However, trees and shrubs grow from their tips and once they have been eaten back, may not be able to branch and continue growing. But grasses grow from their bases. Getting the tops of their leaves eaten is no problem because they'll just keep growing from the ground level. Some grasses even grow more vigorously if their tops are eaten every once in a while.

Okay … So let's say that the trees and shrubs manage to grow in spite of little water and grazing animals. Well, after a long, dry, and sometimes hot summer on the grasslands, wildfires may start. These fast-moving fires, fanned by the winds that commonly blow across these broad, open areas, burn all the dry vegetation in their path. If a tree is large, the fire may move past so quickly that the tree survives. But small trees and young bushes can easily be killed. Some grasses are also killed by wildfire, but many survive because they sprout from the base after a fire has passed. Several species also have underground stems called rhizomes that will sprout again once the fire is past and water and warm weather return.

Side-oats Grama

What if you're an animal living on the grasslands? Many of the animals here live in underground burrows. A type of owl called the **burrowing owl** escapes the drying wind and predators by living underground. And burrows also provide a safe place to escape wildfires. Some birds that usually nest in trees or tall bushes such as **mourning doves,** will nest on the ground if something taller is not available.

The openness of the grasslands makes it hard for large animals to hide from predators, but easier for predators to see their prey. Some, like the **pronghorn** and **deer**, rely on speed to escape. Others, like the **swift fox**, rely on their speed to catch prey.

These wonderful areas where the sky meets the grass cover more of the earth's surface than any other biome. Full of life and adventure, they are waiting to be explored.

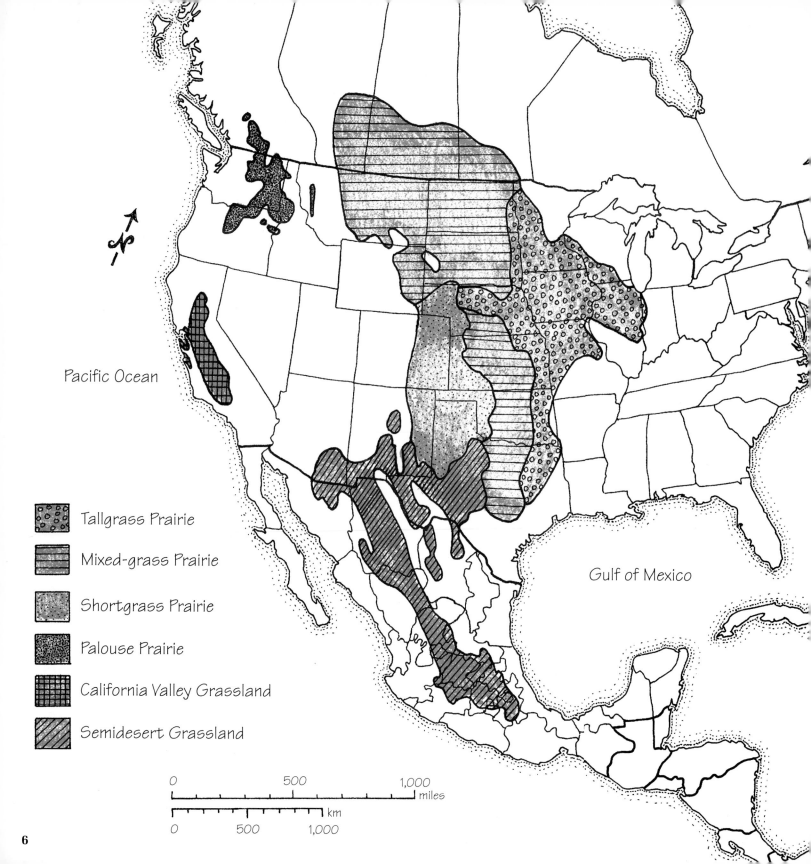

Pacific Ocean

Gulf of Mexico

Tallgrass Prairie

Mixed-grass Prairie

Shortgrass Prairie

Palouse Prairie

California Valley Grassland

Semidesert Grassland

0        500        1,000
                          miles

0        500        1,000
                     km

# North American Prairies and Grasslands

There are many different kinds of grassland regions in North America. This book deals with six major ones: the tallgrass prairie, mixed-grass prairie, shortgrass prairie, Palouse prairie, California Valley Grassland and Semidesert grassland.

Pasque flower

The largest area of grasslands is in the center of North America in an area called the Great Plains. In this "sea of grass," the wind moves the grass like ripples across the ocean, and in some areas there is rolling grassland as far as the eye can see. When European travelers first saw this area more than 300 years ago, they gave it the name "prérie," which means meadow, grassland or grassy orchard. The spelling was later changed to "prairie," and it is here you'll find the tallgrass, mixed-grass, and shortgrass prairies.

As settlers moved onto the prairies and other grasslands, their food crops replaced many of the native grasses and plants, while their cattle and sheep grazed on much of the remaining areas. Slowly, the plants and animals of the North American prairies and grasslands disappeared until very few remained. But things have been changing. People have started studying grassland life and are working to preserve what is left. In some cases, land that had been used for farming or grazing is being restored to prairie. This book has information about some of the most commonly seen plants and animals of both the original and restored prairies and grasslands so you can find them yourself.

Prairie Falcon

One of the most important things to learn before your trip to a grassland is the plant or animal's habitat. **Bison** and **black-tailed prairie dogs** live on flat or rolling grasslands. **Cottonwoods** and **willows** need lots of water, so they will be in riparian areas alongside streams and rivers.

Amphibians like **tiger salamanders** and **frogs** will be in other riparian areas such as marshes, ponds, and hogwallows. Cliffs or high rocky outcrops may provide nesting areas for birds of prey such as **prairie falcons** and **red-tailed hawks**. **Deer** seek the cover of woody draws and **sunflowers** grow along disturbed ground and road edges.

Another important thing to learn is when to look for some plants and animals since they may only occur or be easy to spot during a certain season of the year. The **pasqueflower** is one of the first plants to bloom in the spring, so you will not find it later in the year. And to see **big bluestem** at its tallest height of 6–9 feet (1.8–2.7 m), you have to visit in the fall, after it's been growing for several months. As you look at the two-page drawing found in each grassland section, springtime is on the left-hand side of the drawing, summer is in the middle, and fall is on the right-hand side. Winter in the grasslands is not included because many of the plants have died back and many of the animals have either migrated to warmer areas or are asleep in burrows until spring.

Use this book to enjoy learning about one of the world's most amazing biomes.

Monarch

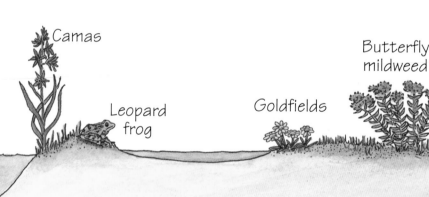

Cottonwood

Camas

Butterfly mildweed

Sandhill crane

Leopard frog

Goldfields

Walleye

### RIPARIAN

**Riparian** areas have water all year long, either on the surface such as in streams and ponds, or hidden underground. Deer and other animals may be found hiding among the willows and birds may perch or nest in the trees. Large riparian areas with surface water also attract migrating birds.

### HOGWALLOWS and VERNAL POOLS

Small pools that fill up with winter or spring rain and don't drain are called **hogwallows** or **vernal pools**. They provide a home for frogs and other amphibians and may become surrounded by wildflowers before they've evaporated by summer.

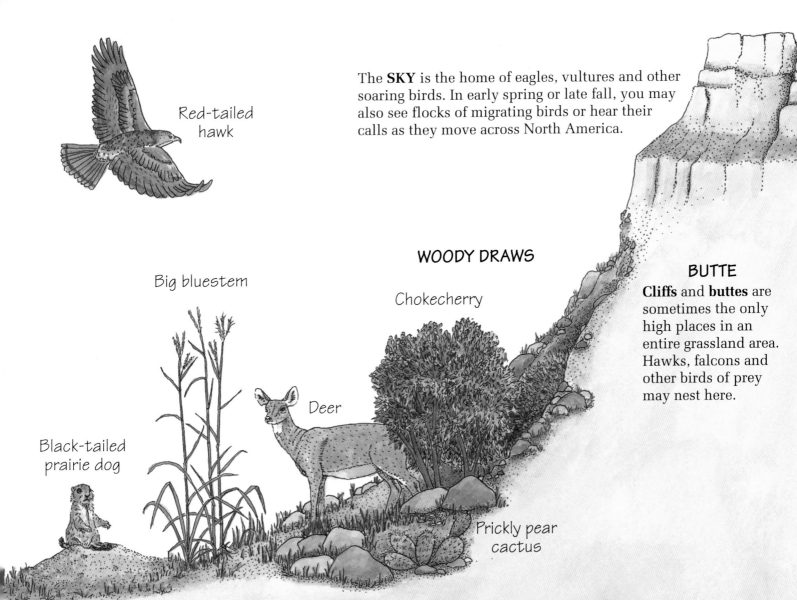

Red-tailed hawk

The **SKY** is the home of eagles, vultures and other soaring birds. In early spring or late fall, you may also see flocks of migrating birds or hear their calls as they move across North America.

**WOODY DRAWS**

Big bluestem

Chokecherry

**BUTTE**

**Cliffs** and **buttes** are sometimes the only high places in an entire grassland area. Hawks, falcons and other birds of prey may nest here.

Deer

Black-tailed prairie dog

Prickly pear cactus

Woody draws are small, dry canyons that were formed by water. Shrubs and small trees may be found here, protected from the drying wind. Woody draws are also good places for animals to hide and make their homes.

**PLAINS**

The **plains** are the flat or rolling hills of the grassland. Prairie dog towns are found here along with **bison** and other grazing animals.

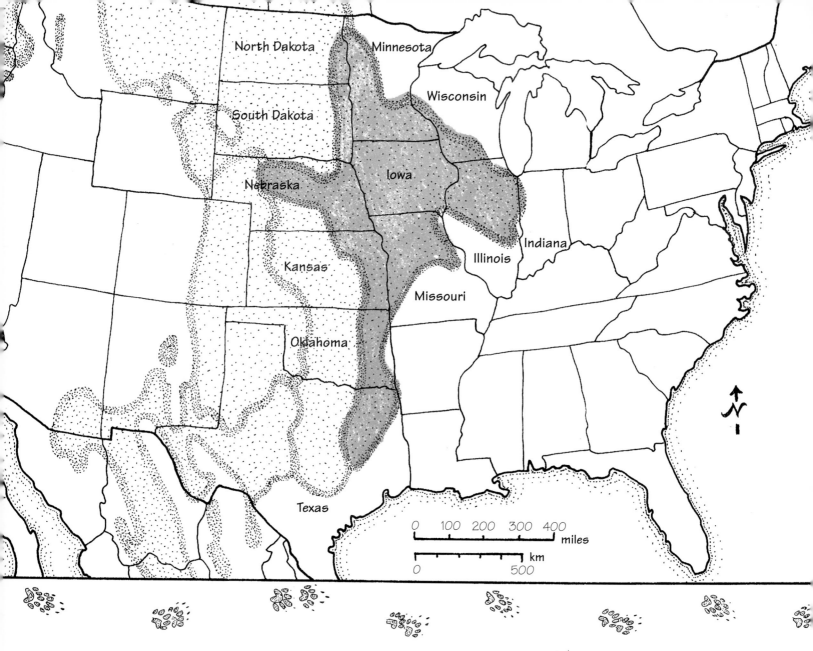

## Great Plains Pocket Gopher

Actually, this very common animal is not only hard to find, it's practically impossible to find. It lives underground its entire life, making tunnels and eating things like plant roots. It is an important food for badgers, snakes and coyotes. One colony of 10 gophers may move 6 tons of dirt per acre (13,605 kg/ha) of land every year. That's a lot of tunnels and gopher mounds!

# Tallgrass Prairie

The light purple flowers of **pasqueflower** showing up among the past year's dry grasses mean that spring has come to the tallgrass prairie. As the weather continues to warm up, you'll find pink **wild roses,** orange **butterfly milkweeds**, purple **blazing stars** and yellow **goldenrods**. At the same time, the grasses of this prairie are sprouting from seeds or underground shoots. As the flowers come and go, the grasses grow taller and taller. Soon it is hard to see anything but grasses. By late summer, the tallgrass prairie lives up to its name with grasses like **big bluestem** and **Indian grass** as high as 9 feet (2.7 m) tall.

These grasses are tall primarily because of the rainfall, which is greater here than in the other grasslands of North America, and the fertile soil. Years ago, when pioneers came onto the tallgrass prairie from the forests of eastern North America, they found it a very good place to raise their crops and graze their animals. Soon, all that was left of this grassland was "islands" of prairie among farmland, pastures, roads and cities.

Fritillary and
Bird's Foot Violet

Big Bluestem

Today people are preserving the remaining tallgrass prairie and restoring other areas to native grassland. Seeds are collected from native tallgrass species and planted on land that is no longer used for farming or grazing. As the tallgrass prairie expands, prairie plants and animals are easier to find. Along the edge of woody areas, you might see **fritillary butterflies** flying among **bird's foot violets** in the spring. This is also where you might see **white-tailed deer** and rabbits called **cottontails**.

In the more open areas, look for the wildflowers called **rattlesnake master** and **compass plant**. Rattlesnake master was thought to be an antidote to the poisonous bite of rattlesnakes. And compass plant, a relative of sunflowers, has leaves that point north and south, like a compass.

If you visit this spectacular prairie, try to come twice—once in the spring for the beginning of the wildflowers and again in the late summer to see the tallest of the grasses and the incredible sunflowers. This is a prairie not to be missed.

# TALLGRASS PRAIRIE

Cottonwood

Giant swallowtail

Eastern kingbird

Wild plum

Monarch butterfly

Coyote

Butterfly milkweed

Smooth sumac

Switchgrass

Blazing star

Meadowlark

Red-winged blackbird

Pale purple coneflower

Painted turtle

Gartersnake

Striped skunk

Canada wild rye

Prairie vole

Tiger salamander

Largemouth bass

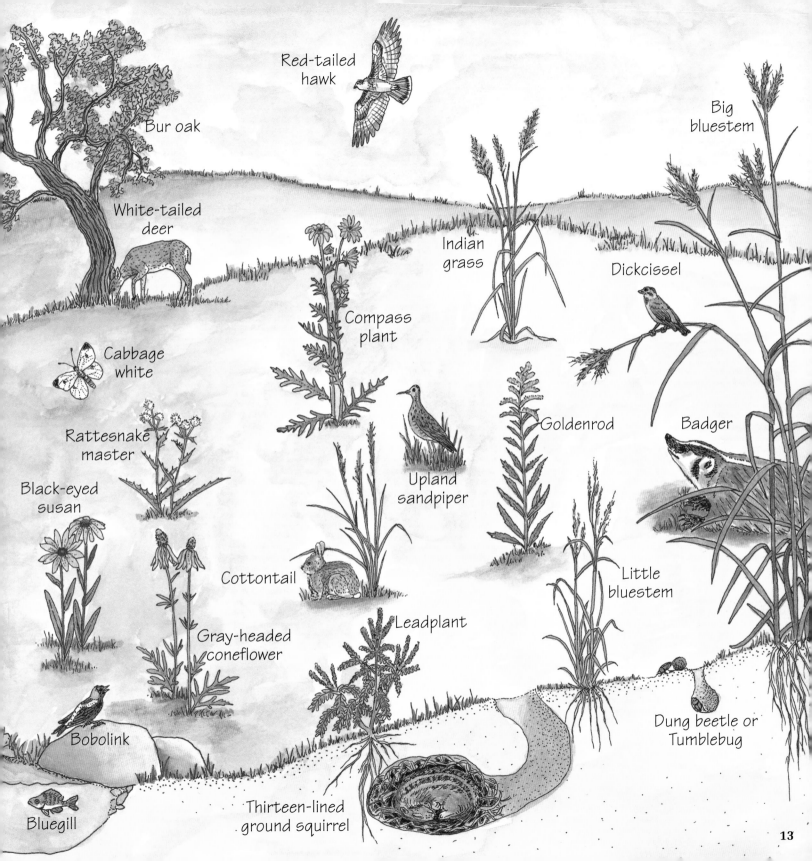

Red-tailed hawk

Bur oak

Big bluestem

White-tailed deer

Indian grass

Dickcissel

Compass plant

Cabbage white

Rattesnake master

Goldenrod

Badger

Black-eyed susan

Upland sandpiper

Cottontail

Little bluestem

Gray-headed coneflower

Leadplant

Dung beetle or Tumblebug

Bobolink

Bluegill

Thirteen-lined ground squirrel

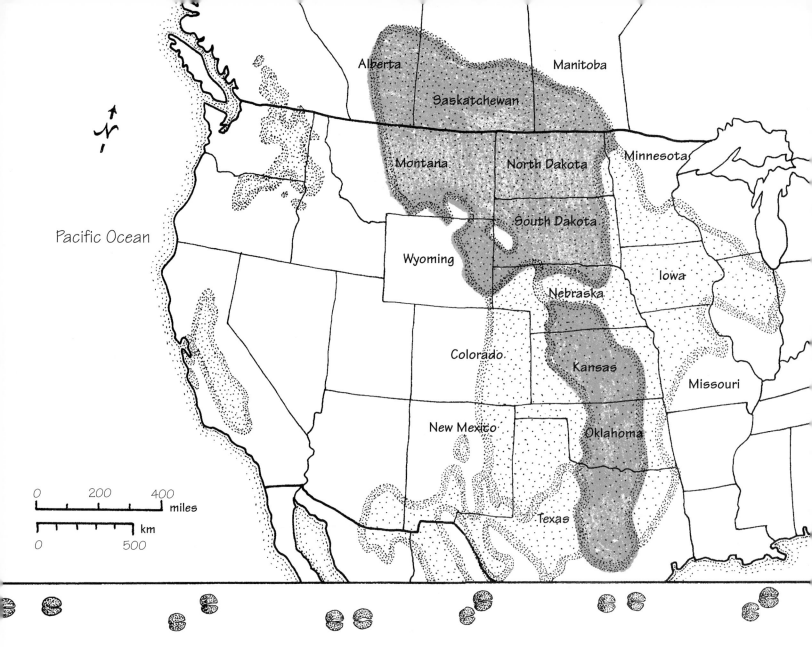

Pacific Ocean

Alberta
Saskatchewan
Manitoba
Montana
North Dakota
Minnesota
South Dakota
Wyoming
Iowa
Nebraska
Colorado
Kansas
Missouri
New Mexico
Oklahoma
Texas

0    200    400 miles

0    500 km

# HARD TO FIND

## Burying Beetle

This large black and orange beetle finds animals like birds or mice
that have died. It then digs the dirt out from under the animal,
burying it. But before covering it up, the beetle lays eggs near the
animal's body. Several days later, the eggs hatch and the young
beetles are fed from the dead animal.

# Mixed-grass Prairie

This is a prairie with enough rainfall in some areas to support tallgrass species, very little rainfall in other areas so that only shortgrass species grow, and still other areas with just enough water to support plants of an in-between size. That is why it's called the "mixed-grass" prairie. It is also the grassland with the most *plant diversity,* or different types of plants. And although there were **bison** on all the prairies many years ago, it is on the mixed-grass prairie where they seem to have reached their greatest numbers.

Woodhouse's Toad

This is a prairie of gently rolling hills with scattered uplands and low-lying areas. The average plant height is about 3 feet (1 m) and very little bare ground is visible. So finding some of the smaller plants and animals can be difficult, especially in summer when most of the vegetation has reached its full size. Learn to watch carefully and listen to the sounds all around you.

If you are near still water and you hear what sounds like a sheep being choked, it's probably **Woodhouse's toad**. These large toads can range in color from yellow to green or brown and are sometimes found at night near the lights from buildings as they try to catch insects.

Another animal on the mixed-grass prairie that eats insects is a small bird called the **grasshoppper sparrow**. If you look carefully, you're most likely to find this brown and tan bird

Grasshopper Sparrow and Little Bluestem

on the ground in areas with **little bluestem** grass and **yucca**. You might think

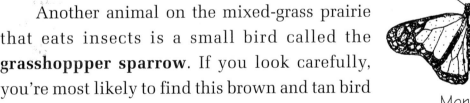
Monarch

it gets its name from the way it hops around or the grasshoppers it may eat, but its name actually comes from its buzzy, grasshopper-like song.

As you walk through this area, try to spot butterflies—the healthier the prairie, the more kinds of butterflies. Some of the large, common butterflies to look for are the orange and black **monarch**, the yellow and black **tiger swallowtail** and the white **cabbage white**.

Visiting the mixed-grass prairie is a bit like taking a trip back in time to when herds of bison thundered across the plains. Listen … you can almost hear them coming.

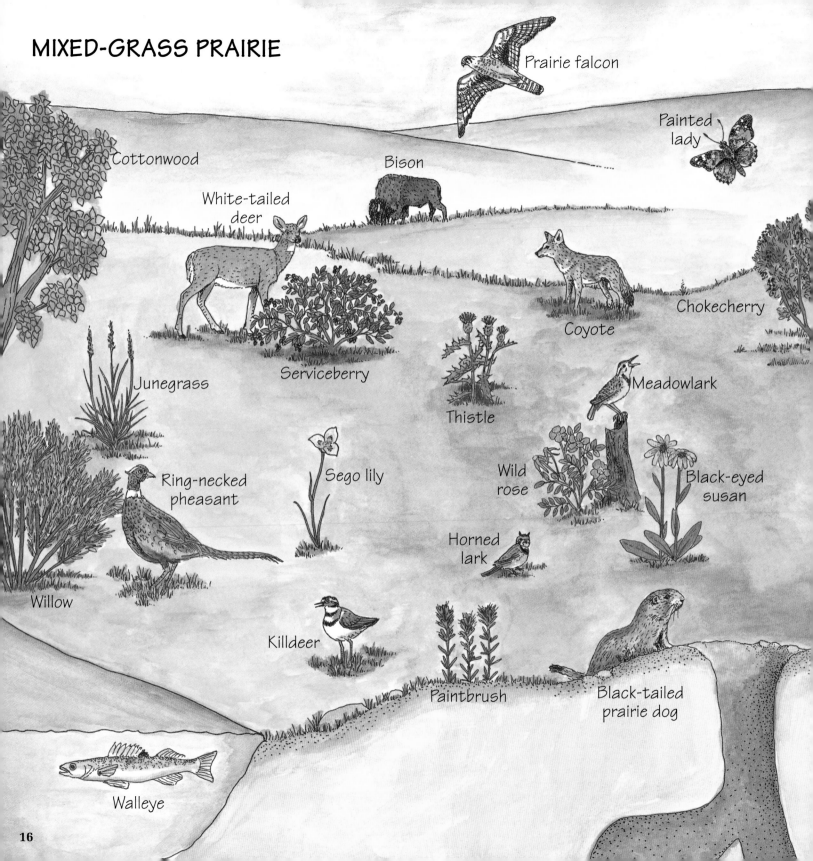

# MIXED-GRASS PRAIRIE

Prairie falcon

Painted lady

Cottonwood

Bison

White-tailed deer

Coyote

Chokecherry

Serviceberry

Junegrass

Thistle

Meadowlark

Sego lily

Ring-necked pheasant

Wild rose

Black-eyed susan

Horned lark

Willow

Killdeer

Paintbrush

Black-tailed prairie dog

Walleye

American
kestrel

Pronghorn

Mule deer

Common
sunflower

Big sagebrush

Prickly
poppy

Prickly pear

Rattlesnake

Yucca

Salsify

Badger

Blue grama

Sideoats
grama

Little
bluestem

Foxtail
barley

Upland sandpiper

Vervain

Mourning dove

Dung
beetles

Thirteen-lined
ground squirrel

Deer mouse

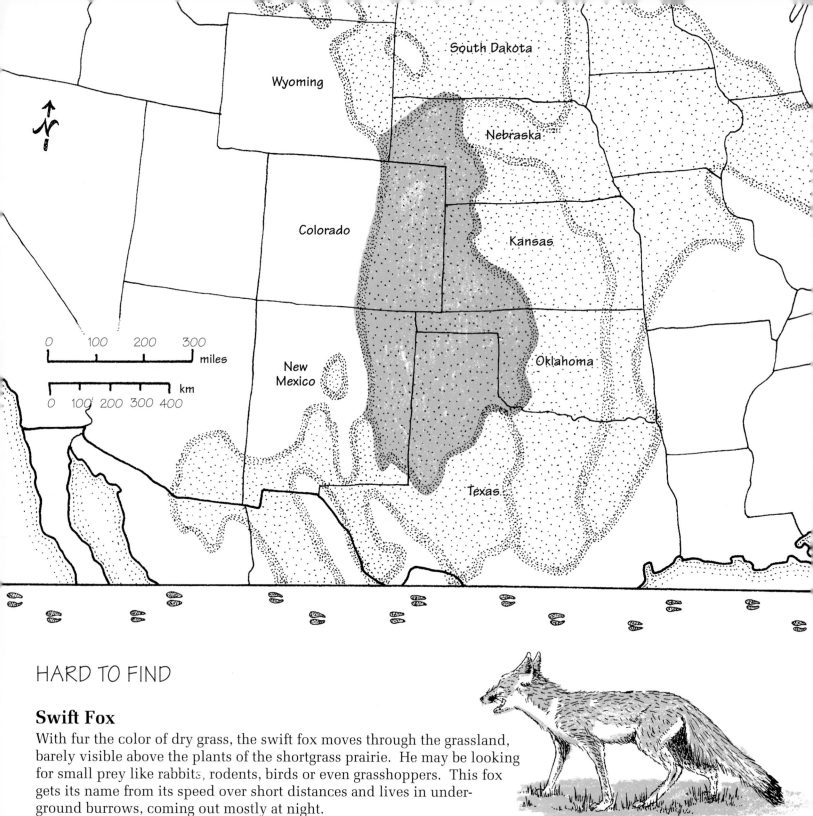

## HARD TO FIND

### Swift Fox

With fur the color of dry grass, the swift fox moves through the grassland, barely visible above the plants of the shortgrass prairie. He may be looking for small prey like rabbits, rodents, birds or even grasshoppers. This fox gets its name from its speed over short distances and lives in underground burrows, coming out mostly at night.

# Shortgrass Prairie

Someone once said that you'll know you're in shortgrass prairie when you can throw a baseball into the grassland and still see the ball after it lands. And while this is not true of all areas in the shortgrass prairie, it would probably work in most of them. The plants of this prairie usually grow no higher than your knees and are separated by patches of bare ground. Of all the North American prairies, this is the driest with long periods of drought and hot weather. The Rocky Mountains stop most of the rain coming from the Pacific Ocean from reaching the shortgrass prairie. This puts the shortgrass prairie in the "rainshadow" of the Rocky Mountains and is the main reason for the dry climate.

Rocky Mountain
Bee Plant

In a way this is a good thing, because it makes it easier to spot most of the plants and animals that live in this grassland. An easy one to find is the **Rocky Mountain bee plant**. It's about 2–5 feet (0.6–1.5 m) tall and has light purple flowers all summer long. And, although bees like it, the plant stinks. It actually smells so bad that some people who work in the shortgrass prairie keep a piece of it in their cars to repel mosquitoes during the summer.

**Bison** and **pronghorn** are fairly common in the shortgrass prairie. Along with **elk, white-tailed deer** and **mule deer**, they are the primary large animals of this and the other grasslands. Pronghorn are also known as the fastest land animal in North America and can run up to 70 miles (113 km) per hour for a few minutes at a time.

Dung Beetle

Look down among the grasses and you might see some small dark beetles rolling what looks like a round, brown rock across the ground. These are **dung beetles**, one of the most interesting insects of the prairies. That "rock" is actually a ball of dung, or animal poop. The beetles push the dung ball into an underground burrow and lay one of their eggs inside the dung. When the egg hatches, the larva eats the dung. It's good for the beetles because it provides food for the young, and it's good for the prairie because it helps recycle nutrients back into the soil. It also helps prevent the prairie from becoming covered in animal poop!

Easy to walk through, fascinating to explore … that's the shortgrass prairie.

# SHORTGRASS PRAIRIE

Loggerhead shrike

Swainson's hawk

Pronghorn

Small soapweed

Monarch

Cottonwood

Needlegrass

Prickly pear

Western wheatgrass

Showy milkweed

Scarlet globemallow

Rocky Mountain bee plant

American avocet

Meadowlark

Bullsnake

Tiger salamander

Willow

Prairie coneflower

Horned lark

Garter snake

Killdeer

Burrowing owl

Killifish

Leopard frog

Dragonfly

Lubber grasshopper

Horned lizard

Golden eagle

Common sulfur

Bison

Mule deer

Big Sagebrush

Curly dock

Coyote

Harvester ant mound

Rabbitbrush

Blue grama

Common sunflower

Evening primrose

Striped skunk

Yellow sweet clover

Mourning dove

Rattlesnake

Black-tailed prairie dog

Badger

Buffalo grass

Thirteen-lined ground squirrel

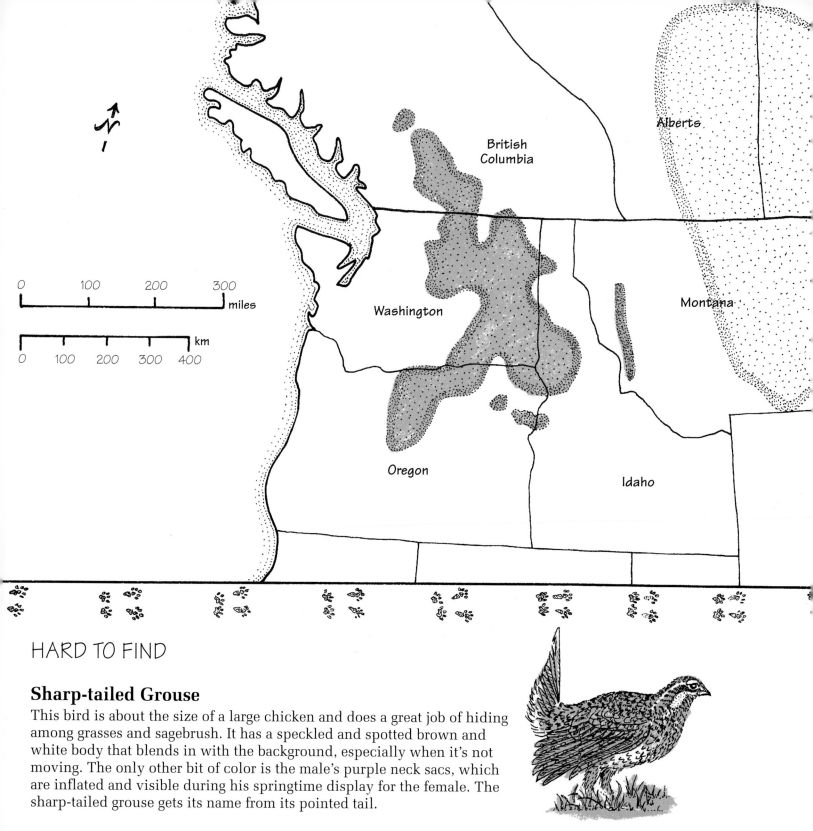

# HARD TO FIND

## Sharp-tailed Grouse

This bird is about the size of a large chicken and does a great job of hiding among grasses and sagebrush. It has a speckled and spotted brown and white body that blends in with the background, especially when it's not moving. The only other bit of color is the male's purple neck sacs, which are inflated and visible during his springtime display for the female. The sharp-tailed grouse gets its name from its pointed tail.

# Palouse Prairie

When French explorers first came upon this land of rolling grassland, they named it "pelouse" (now "palouse"), which means lawn. The Palouse prairie is found between and near the mountains of northwestern North America. This "intermountain" area has a wet winter eventually followed by a

Buffalo Bunchgrass

hot, dry summer. The plants usually grow as high as your knees or waist, about 1–3 feet (0.3–1.0 m) high, similar to those on the mixed-grass prairie. Many areas of the Palouse prairie are covered almost entirely by grasses with very few shrubs and even fewer trees. The most common grasses found here are referred to as "cool-season" bunch grasses, such as **buffalo bunchgrass** and **bluebunch wheatgrass**. That means that these grasses grow only as clumps and do almost all of their growing during the cooler springtime.

From late spring to early summer, **arrowleaf balsam root** is in flower. It is related to sunflowers and covers large areas with bright yellow blooms. The "arrowleaf" part of its name comes from the arrowhead shape of its leaves. The aboveground part of the plant is eaten by **deer** and **elk**. The carrotlike roots were eaten by Native Americans.

Bitter Cherry

Another plant eaten by deer and elk is the **bitter cherry**. This shrub gets its name from its bitter taste and from the bright red fruits during the fall that look like small cherries. But that's not all—when you scrape the smooth, thin bark, it even *smells* like cherries!

Narrow trails through the grass may be a sign that **meadow voles** live nearby. These small animals are usually out at night (nocturnal) and look like fat, brown mice with short tails and small ears. And while you're looking for meadow voles, you might also want to look for the **coyotes,** snakes and hawks that feed on these little rodents.

Farming and pastureland have replaced most of the Palouse prairie. But many of the plants and animals can still be found if you know where to look.

Meadow Vole

# PALOUSE PRAIRIE

Lupine

Common Sulfur

Douglas fir

Red-tailed hawk

Bison

Ornate tiger moth

Junegrass

Buffalo bunchgrass

Coyote

Meadowlark

Sandhill crane

Owl's clover

Killdeer

Bluebunch wheatgrass

Northern harrier

Arrowleaf balsam root

Camas

Wild rose

Tiger salamander

Spotted frog

Ladybug

24

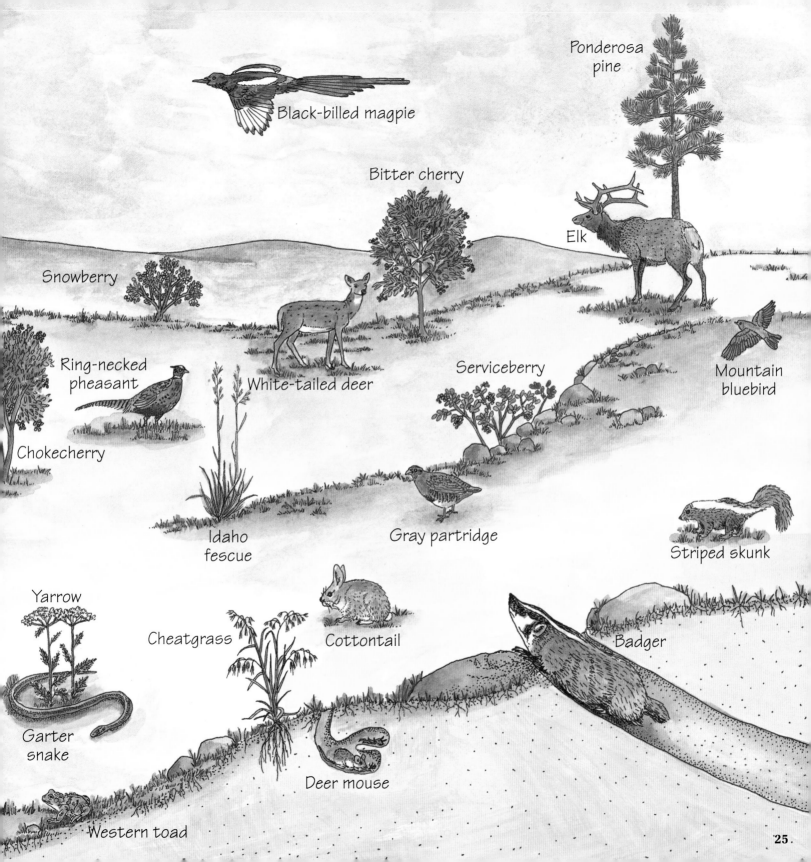

Black-billed magpie

Ponderosa pine

Bitter cherry

Elk

Snowberry

Ring-necked pheasant

White-tailed deer

Serviceberry

Mountain bluebird

Chokecherry

Idaho fescue

Gray partridge

Striped skunk

Yarrow

Cheatgrass

Cottontail

Badger

Garter snake

Deer mouse

Western toad

**25**

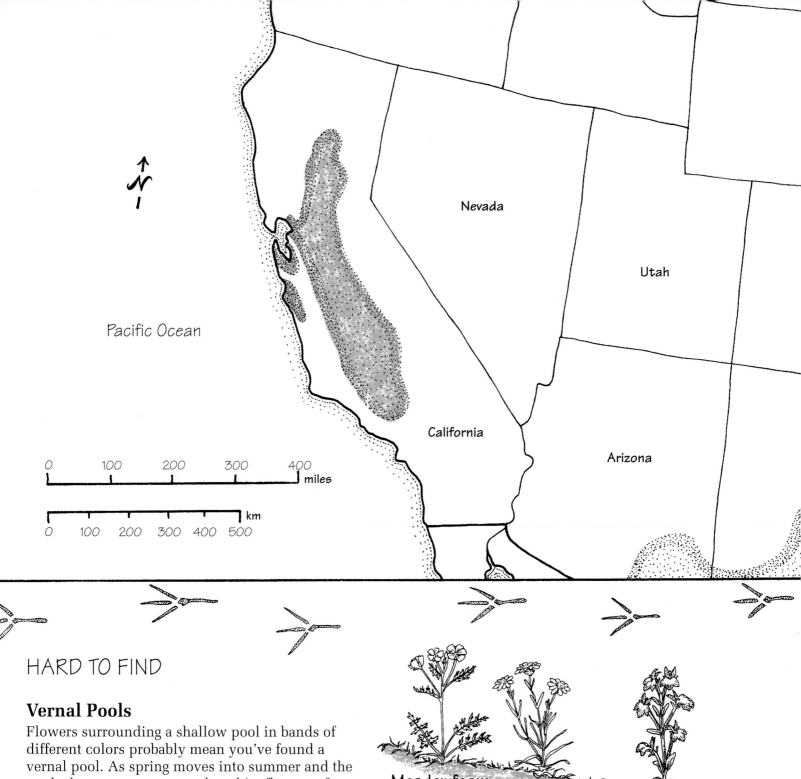

# HARD TO FIND

## Vernal Pools

Flowers surrounding a shallow pool in bands of different colors probably mean you've found a vernal pool. As spring moves into summer and the pools dry up, you may see the white flowers of meadowfoam, then yellow goldfields and finally the deep bluish purple and white flowers of downingia.

**Meadowfoam**   **Goldfields**   **Downingia**

# California Valley Grassland

The Spanish missionaries and settlers of California must have been amazed when they came here more than 200 years ago. **Mountain lions** and **grizzly bears** roamed the valley grassland in search of **elk** and **pronghorn**. **Purple needlegrass** and other grasses extended from the marshes of the lowlands to the dry mountain foothills. Springtime displays of colorful wildflowers like yellow **goldfields** and orange **California poppy** would cover such large areas that it looked as if a giant had spilled paint over the flatlands and foothills.

Wild Oats

These new settlers brought their own crops and animals into the area as well. Sometimes weed seeds were brought in too, hidden among the crop seeds or stuck in the fur of animals. These introduced plants and animals did very well in California—too well. Eventually many of the native plants were replaced by introduced plants such as **wild oats** and **curly dock**. Many of the native animals that were not killed by hunting moved away as their habitats changed or disappeared. Although there are places where native species still occur, only 1% of the original California Valley Grassland remains.

Kangaroo Rat

**Tule elk**, the smallest elk in North America, can still be found here. A good place to see them is the San Luis National Wildlife Refuge in the central part of the grassland. They were named after the **tule reeds** that grow along edges of the shallow lakes and ponds. Perched on the ends of the tule reeds, may be **red-winged blackbirds,** and flying low over the ground nearby, **northern harriers** may be hunting for frogs, mice and other small animals.

Winter rains usually mean you'll find springtime wildflowers like blue **lupines** and yellow **tidy-tips** in fields and on hillsides. These are followed in late spring and early summer by pale yellow carpets of **mustard**, an introduced plant. Look along the ground for signs of the very common **pocket gopher,** digging up the earth and leaving behind mounds of fresh dirt.

With its incredible wildflower displays and pockets of preserved grassland, the California Valley Grassland is a wonderful place to explore.

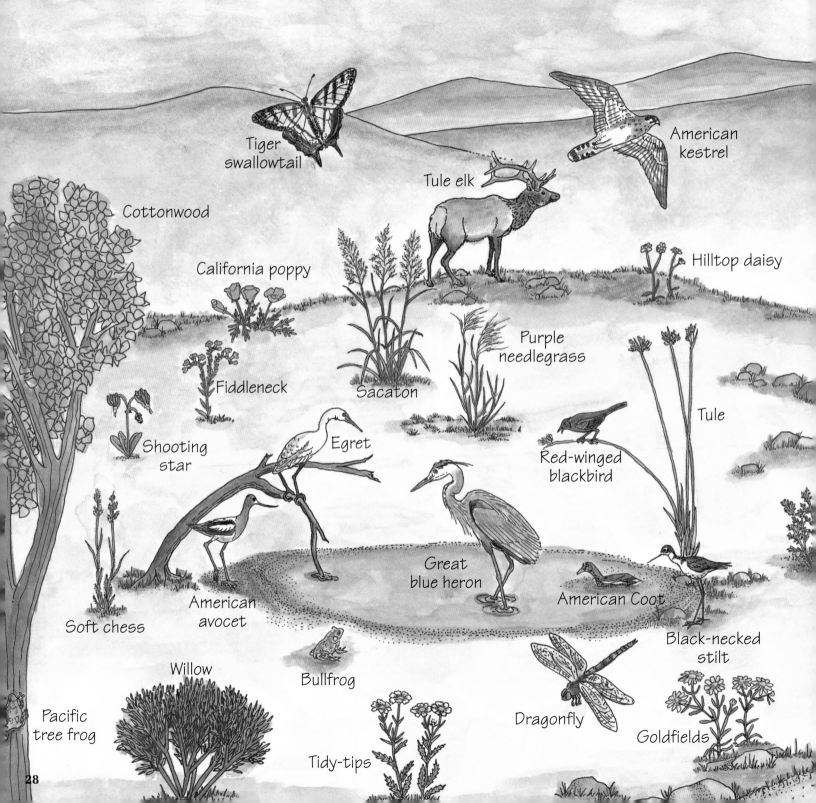

Tiger swallowtail

American kestrel

Tule elk

Cottonwood

Hilltop daisy

California poppy

Purple needlegrass

Fiddleneck

Sacaton

Tule

Shooting star

Egret

Red-winged blackbird

Soft chess

American avocet

Great blue heron

American Coot

Black-necked stilt

Pacific tree frog

Willow

Bullfrog

Dragonfly

Goldfields

Tidy-tips

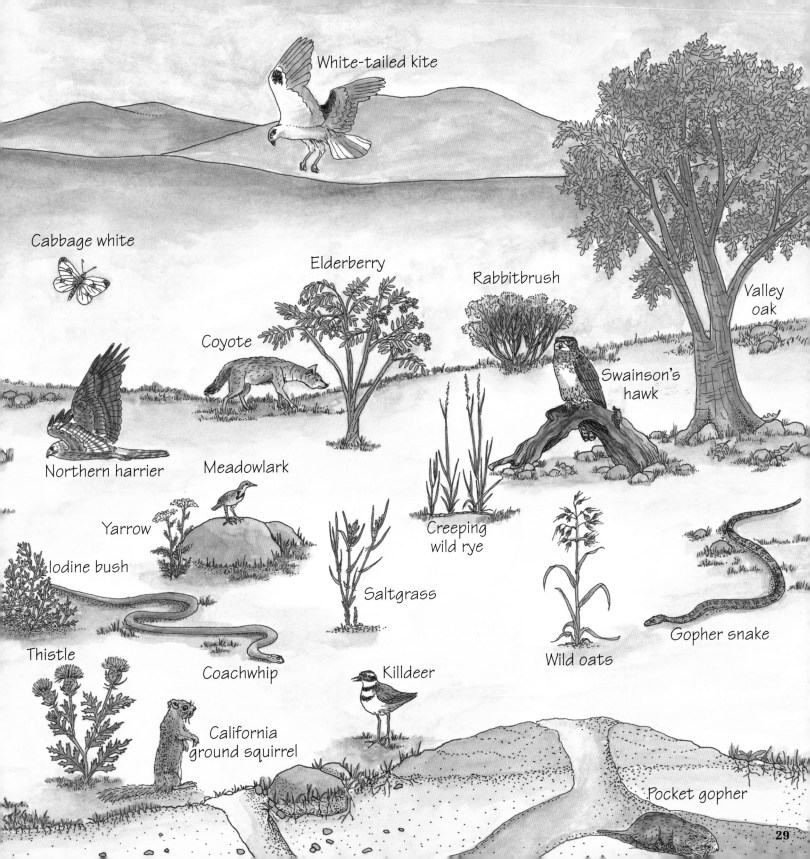

White-tailed kite

Cabbage white

Elderberry

Rabbitbrush

Valley oak

Coyote

Swainson's hawk

Northern harrier

Meadowlark

Yarrow

Iodine bush

Creeping wild rye

Saltgrass

Gopher snake

Thistle

Coachwhip

Killdeer

Wild oats

California ground squirrel

Pocket gopher

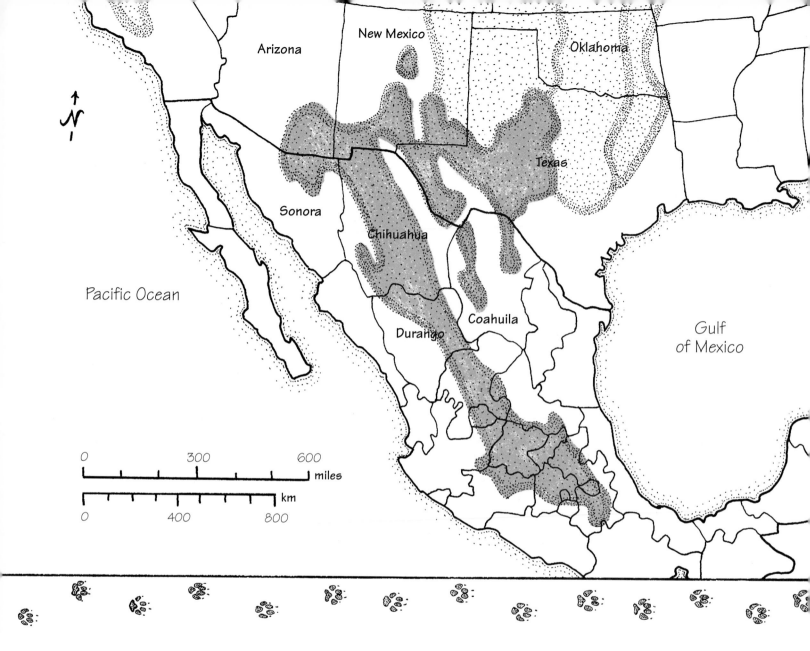

Arizona

New Mexico

Oklahoma

Texas

Sonora

Chihuahua

Pacific Ocean

Coahuila

Durango

Gulf
of Mexico

| 0 | 300 | 600 |
|---|-----|-----|

miles

km

| 0 | 400 | 800 |
|---|-----|-----|

## HARD TO FIND

### Living Rock Cactus

This cactus is dull gray or brown in color and looks very much like the dry, rocky habitat where it lives. Also, it barely grows above the surface of the ground, making it even harder to find. The easiest time to spot it is when it has flowers. These flowers can be up to $1^{1}/_{2}$ inches (4 cm) across and are colored a very bright, hot pink. It grows in the eastern part of the semidesert grassland.

# Semidesert Grassland

This is the hottest, driest and sunniest of all the grasslands in North America. It is spread out in the basins and valleys between the lower, drier desert and the higher foothills and mountains in the southwestern United States and northern Mexico. Summer is the hottest time, when the temperature can reach 100°F (37.4°C) or more. Summer is also when most of the rain falls here, averaging about 15 inches (38.1 cm) per year. That's only a few inches more than in the nearby desert. This is part of the reason that plants here are fairly short and spread out with lots of empty space in between.

Wait-a-Minute Bush

But even with all the short plants and empty space, it's not always easy to walk through this grassland. Many of the cacti, succulents, shrubs and other plants have spines or thorns. The **catclaw** gets its name from the many small curved thorns along its branches, and the **white thorn's** long, straight white spines are easy to spot against the shrub's reddish brown bark. **Prickly pear cactus** has spines with barbs on them that are especially hard to pull out if they get in your skin. And look out for thickets of the **wait-a-minute bush,** which will hook your clothes (or your skin!) and cause you to "wait a minute" while you unhook yourself. This bush's white and pink or purplish flowers attract insects such as bees, wasps and butterflies.

Windscorpion

Wildlife may be visible, especially if it's not too hot. If you catch a glimpse of a long, narrow, pinkish red snake moving very quickly across the ground, it's probably a **red racer**. It is a type of coachwhip, one of the fastest snakes in the world. **Turkey vultures** may be along the road eating "roadkill," animals that were accidentally killed by cars and other moving vehicles during the night. Want to see **tarantulas**? Visit in the fall when male tarantulas are out walking around looking for females.

Some of the animals of this grassland are nocturnal, coming out at night. That's when you might find the fast **windscorpions**. They look like something between a spider and a scorpion, and use their huge jaws to crush and tear apart their prey. Since they occur in dry, sunny places like the desert, they are also known as "sunspiders." Windscorpions are not poisonous but they can pinch hard, so be careful.

The best time to visit this grassland may be in the late summer after most of the rain has fallen. But whenever you visit, you'll see many plants and animals unlike those in any of the other grasslands. Just watch out for those plant spines and thorns!

# SEMIDESERT GRASSLAND

Swainson's Hawk

Coyote

Yucca moth

Agave

Palo Verde

Soaptree Yucca

Lupine

Jackrabbit

Vermilion flycatcher

Purple prickly pear

Lehmann lovegrass

Greater roadrunner

Gopher snake

Scaled quail

Sacaton

Barrel Cactus

Lark bunting

Javelina

Kangaroo rat

Bandwinged grasshopper

Whiptail lizard

Red-tailed hawk

Turkey vulture

Sotol

Mesquite

Pronghorn

Mule deer

Bush muhly

White thorn

Catclaw

Devil's claw

Burrowgrass

Massasauga

Snakeweed

Tobosa

Box turtle

Horselubber grasshopper

Stink beetle

Tarantula

Fire ant

Horned lizard

Harvester ant

33

# Common Plants and Animals

Some of the plants and animals are so common that they can be found on more than one grassland. **Meadowlarks** and **coyotes**, for example, occur on all the grasslands. This does not mean that you will see all of these plants and animals each time you visit a grassland area, but the chances are pretty good that you'll see one or more of them.

Information next to the drawings will help you learn what to look for and where to look. Remember that the time of year you visit the grassland is important, too. Spring, summer and early fall are the best times to see most of the plants of the grasslands because that is when they are growing and flowering. And many animals are active early in the day when the air is cool, especially during the spring and early summer.

Learn to look carefully and listen well. You may be surprised to discover things you never knew were there.

## COYOTE
**Color:** Light brown, gray, and white.
**Size:** 3–4 feet (1–1.2 m) long. About the size of a large dog.
**Food:** Omnivorous, eating almost anything.
**Notes:** Coyotes are sometimes seen in open grassland during the day but usually spend that time in underground burrows. Listen for their "yipping" calls at night and look for them running near roads. Their light-colored fur shows up well in car headlights at night but blends in with the dead grasses of late summer and fall during the day. The coyote is the state animal of South Dakota.

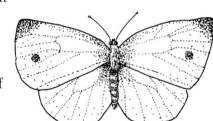

## CABBAGE WHITE
**Color:** White with 1-2 dark spots on wings.
**Size:** 1–2 inch (2.5–5 cm) wingspan.
**Food:** Flower nectar. Larvae eat wild mustard plants.
**Notes:** This common butterfly was introduced from Europe around 1860. It is now found all over North America.

## GARTER SNAKE
**Color:** Tan, brown, black or greenish. All have a stripe, usually whitish or yellow, running down their back, and most have another stripe on each side of their body.
**Size:** Up to 4 feet (1.2 m) long.
**Food:** Frogs, toads, small fishes, earthworms and sometimes other reptiles.
**Notes:** Look for most garter snakes in or near water. They are out during the day, sunning themselves or hunting for food.

## MEADOWLARK

**Color:** Wide, black band in the shape of a "V" on bright yellow breast. Mottled brown back.

**Size:** 8–11 inches (20.3–28 cm) long.

**Food:** Insects, berries and seeds.

**Notes:** Look for them in open fields and grasslands. They can often be seen with their head tilted back and singing while sitting on a fence post or tree stump. The western meadowlark is the state bird of Kansas, Montana, Nebraska, North Dakota, Oregon and Wyoming.

## COMMON SUNFLOWER

**Color:** Yellow flowers, sometimes with dark brown centers, and dark green leaves and stems.

**Size:** 2–10 feet (0.6–3.0 m) high.

**Notes:** These wildflowers are found all summer long in the prairies and grasslands and are often found alongside roads. The common sunflower is the state flower of Kansas.

## TIGER SALAMANDER

**Color:** Usually dark brown or blackish with large, light-colored spots or blotches.

**Size:** 3–13 inches (7.6–33.0 cm) long. Average size is about 7 inches (17.8 cm) long.

**Food:** Insects and worms.

**Notes:** Tiger salamanders are usually in underground burrows or under leaves and other objects at the water's edge. Look for them when they come out at night just after spring or summer rains. The state amphibian of Kansas is the tiger salamander.

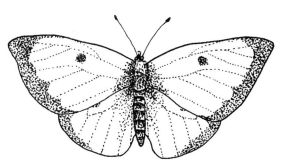

## SULFUR

**Color:** Pale yellow to bright orange. Some have dark wing edges.

**Size:** 1$\frac{1}{2}$–2$\frac{1}{2}$ inch (3.8–6.4 cm) wingspan.

**Food:** Nectar from flowers. Larvae eat wildflowers such as clover, vetch and lupine.

**Notes:** The bright color of these butterflies makes them easy to spot, especially when they're flying.

# Birds

## UPLAND SANDPIPER
**Color:** Tan and mottled brown with yellow legs.
**Size:** About 12 inches (30.5 cm) tall.
**Food:** Insects.
**Notes:** Easy to spot when sitting on tree stumps and fence posts, but when it is on the ground among the grasses, only its head may be visible. Look for it in the northern Great Plains.

## LARK BUNTING

**Color:** Males are black with white patch on wings; females are streaked with grayish brown.
**Size:** 5$^1$/$_2$–7$^1$/$_2$ inches (14.0–19 cm) long.
**Food:** Mostly grasshoppers, beetles and seeds.
**Notes:** Found on the drier prairies and grasslands, often in large groups along the roadside. The lark bunting is the state bird of Colorado.

## SWAINSON'S HAWK
**Color:** Brown with white or rusty brown on lower breast. May also be all brown.
**Size:** 18–22 inches (45.7–55.9 cm) long.
**Food:** Rodents and grasshoppers.
**Notes:** Found in the drier grasslands, sometimes perched on fence posts or rocks. It looks like it is "wobbling" when it's soaring overhead.

## KILLDEER
**Color:** Brown back and white breast with two black bands or stripes across upper breast. Black, white and brown head.
**Size:** 9–11 inches (22–30 cm) long.
**Food:** Insects.
**Notes:** Easy to spot because of their habit of running across open ground, stopping suddenly, then running again. Look for killdeer in meadows, in parks and on shores of rivers and lakes.

## RED-WINGED BLACKBIRD

**Color:** Males are black with red shoulders, females are brown with white and brown streaks on their breast.
**Size:** 8–9 inches (20.3–22.9 cm) long.
**Food:** Insects and seeds.
**Notes:** Common in marshy areas, perched on tall grasses and other plants at the water's edge.

## HORNED LARK

**Color:** Tan back, black stripe across a yellowish breast and black "horns" on their head.
**Size:** About 7 inches (17.8 cm) long.
**Food:** Seeds and insects.
**Notes:** Look for them walking on the ground, sometimes in groups. They are especially easy to spot alongside roads.

# Insects

### LUBBER GRASSHOPPER
**Color:** Tan with greenish areas or black with yellow accents.
**Size:** 1$^1$/$_2$–2$^1$/$_2$ inches (3.8–6.4 cm) long.
**Food:** Leaves and other plant parts.
**Notes:** There are many different kinds of grasshoppers on the prairies and grasslands. Look for them among plants.

### BEES
**Color:** Yellow or amber with black or brown.
**Size:** $^1$/$_2$–1 inch (1.3–2.5 cm) long.
**Food:** Flower nectar and pollen.
**Notes:** Honey bees and bumble bees help pollinate grassland plants. Look for them on wildflowers and flowering grasses in all the grasslands. The honey bee is the state insect of Kansas, Missouri, Nebraska and South Dakota.

### MONARCH
**Color:** Dark orange with black veins and black wing margins, light orange underneath.
**Size:** 3$^1$/$_2$–4$^1$/$_2$ inches wide.
**Food:** Nectar from flowers. Larvae eat milkweeds.
**Notes:** Look for them in the spring and fall when huge numbers of monarchs migrate across North America. The monarch is the official state insect of Illinois.

### DRAGONFLIES
**Color:** Although most are brown, the green darner has a green and bluish body and the common white tail is dark brown and white.
**Size:** 2–3 inches (5.0–7.6 cm) long.
**Food:** Flying insects such as mosquitoes.
**Notes:** Dragonflies are common near water where they may rest at the top of plants growing at the water's edge. The green darner dragonfly is the state insect of Washington.

### DUNG BEETLE
**Color:** Black or dark brown.
**Size:** About $^1$/$_2$ inch (1.3 cm) long.
**Food:** Animal poop or dung.
**Notes:** This beetle helps clean the grasslands by eating dung (animal poop). It is sometimes called a "tumblebug" because it rolls a ball of dung into a small underground burrow, where it lays its eggs.

### HARVESTER ANT
**Color:** Dark brown or reddish brown.
**Size:** $^1$/$_4$–$^1$/$_2$ inch (0.6–1.3 cm) long.
**Food:** Seeds and other plant material.
**Notes:** Look for mounds of fine gravel in the center of a cleared area. Some mounds are so big they may be mistaken for prairie dog mounds from a distance.

# Mammals

## BISON

**Color:** Dark brown.
**Size:** Up to 6 feet (1.8 m) high.
**Food:** Plants, especially grasses.
**Notes:** Active in the early morning and late in the day. The best place to see them is in parks and preserves like Yellowstone National Park and the National Bison Range.

## BLACK-TAILED PRAIRIE DOG

**Color:** Light tan with white underside.
**Size:** 14–16 inches (35.5–41.5 cm) long.
**Food:** Almost any plant near their burrow.
**Notes:** Look for groups of low, volcano-like dirt mounds in flat areas on mixed grass and shortgrass prairie and semidesert grassland. These are the entrances to their burrows. Prairie dogs make short, high-pitched, chirpy calls to warn other prairie dogs of potential danger.

## BADGER

**Color:** Dark brown and white, sometimes with gray on back.
**Size:** 2–3 feet (0.6–1 m) long.
**Food:** Mostly prairie dogs and other small mammals.
**Notes:** Strong front feet and long claws help make it a good burrower. Lives in an underground den in dry, open country and may be out on the grasslands during the day or night.

## THIRTEEN-LINED GROUND SQUIRREL

**Color:** Light brown with white stripes and spots down the back.
**Size:** 8–12 inches (21–30 cm) long, not including the tail.
**Food:** Mostly grasshoppers and plant seeds.
**Notes:** Look for them alongside roads and fences. Their light color and striped pattern help them blend in very well with the dry, roadside plants.

## PRONGHORN

**Color:** White with dark or reddish tan.
**Size:** 4–4¹/₂ feet (1.2–1.4 m) high.
**Food:** Grasses, sagebrush and other plants and their leaves.
**Notes:** Pronghorn are the fastest-running animals in North America. Look for the pronghorn across open areas in the drier grasslands where they are active day or night.

## MULE DEER AND WHITE-TAILED DEER

**Color:** Both white-tailed deer and mule deer are mostly grayish brown with white on their underside. White-tailed deer can also be reddish brown.
**Size:** 4¹/₂–5¹/₂ feet (1.4–1.7 m) high.
**Food:** Grasses, leaves and sometimes twigs of bushes and trees.
**Notes:** Look for deer near the edge of woodlands in the early morning or late afternoon. You might even see them along the edge of the road at night in car headlights. White-tailed deer get their name from the white underside of their tail, which is visible when the deer are running away from danger. Mule deer get their name from their big ears. The white-tailed deer is the state animal of Illinois and Oklahoma, and the state mammal of Nebraska.

# Reptiles, Amphibians and Fish

## HORNED LIZARD
**Color:** Brown, yellowish, tan or some other color that blends in with the lizard's surroundings. May also have dark areas on back.
**Size:** $2^{1}/_{2}$–4 inches (6.4–10.2 cm) long.
**Food:** Ants.
**Notes:** These fat-looking lizards are sometimes called "horned toads." They are found in dry areas with fine-grained dirt and sometimes gravel and rocks. Look for them during the day near ant nests.

## RATTLESNAKE
**Color:** Light tan, greenish or dark grayish brown, usually with dark blotches down the length of its back.
**Size:** $1^{1}/_{2}$–5 feet (0.4–1.5 m) long.
**Food:** Small mammals.
**Notes:** Rattlesnakes are often out late in the afternoon, but can be found at all times of the day. Common around dry, rocky areas and near animal burrows. When disturbed, they may shake the end of their tail and "rattle" the hard segments that grow there. All rattlesnakes, even babies, can bite and are poisonous. Do not go near them.

## COACHWHIP
**Color:** Tan, brown, reddish.
**Size:** 3–$6^{1}/_{2}$ feet (1–2 m) long
**Food:** Insects and other small animals such as frogs, lizards, mice and birds.
**Notes:** Some of these snakes are also called "racers" because they are very fast. Look for them during the day in open areas and crossing roads.

## LEOPARD FROG
**Color:** Green, brownish or gray, usually with dark spots.
**Size:** 2–5 inches (5–12.5 cm) long.
**Food:** Insects.
**Notes:** Look for these frogs at night in or near ponds, marshes and other permanent water. They are also found among the plants at the water's edge and in wet meadows.

## COLLARED LIZARD
**Color:** Yellowish brown or yellowish blue with a black and white band around the back of the neck.
**Size:** 8–14 inches (20.3–35.6 cm) long.
**Food:** Insects and small lizards.
**Notes:** Look for them sunning themselves on rocks during the day in the southern Plains and the semidesert grassland. These lizards bite, so be careful around them.

## KILLIFISH
**Color:** Olive green on top, white or yellowish sides and yellow belly. Dark, vertical stripes along body.
**Size:** Up to 5 inches (12.5 cm) long.
**Food:** Small aquatic plants and animals.
**Notes:** Look for these small fish near the edges of shallow streams and ponds in the Great Plains.

# Wildflowers

### PRICKLY PEAR
**Color:** Yellow to yellowish red flowers on green pads. Blooms May to August.
**Size:** About 1 foot (0.3 m) tall.
**Notes:** This cactus plant is common in drier, sunny grassland areas. After the flowers are done blooming, fruits develop in their place. Prickly pear gets its name from these spiny fruits

### THISTLE
**Color:** Light purple, pinkish or yellow flowers. Blooms June to October.
**Size:** Usually 1–5 feet (0.3–1.5 m) tall.
**Notes:** These prickly plants are common along roadsides and moist ditches. Look for it in all the grasslands. Many thistles are introduced.

### PAINTBRUSH
**Color:** Red, white or yellowish flowers. Blooms April to June.
**Size:** Usually 4–12 inches (10.2–30.5 cm) tall.
**Notes:** The white downy paintbrush is a perennial and grows in clumps. The red Indian paintbrush is an annual and grows from a single stem. Both are found in dry and semimoist grassland areas, sometimes among rocks. Indian paintbrush is the state flower of Wyoming.

### WILD ROSE
**Color:** Light to dark pink flowers. Blooms May to August.
**Size:** Up to 3 feet (0.9 m) tall.
**Notes:** Wild roses are most easily found in thickets, either along roadsides or in open woodland areas. The flowers last until about midsummer and are replaced by red berrylike "hips" that contain the flower's fruits. The wild prairie rose is the state flower of Iowa and North Dakota.

## CONEFLOWER

**Color:** Yellow, pink or purplish flowers, often with dark centers. Blooms May to September.

**Size:** 2–5 feet (0.6–1.5 m) tall.

**Notes:** The bright yellow of the prairie coneflower is especially easy to spot alongside roads in shortgrass and mixed grass prairies.

## YARROW

**Color:** White flowers. Blooms May to October.

**Size:** 1/2–3 feet (0.2–0.9 m) tall.

**Notes:** Look for it along roadsides and other open, disturbed areas in most of the grasslands.

## LUPINE

**Color:** Blue or purplish flowers; sometimes white or reddish. Blooms May to August.

**Size:** Usually about 1/2–3 feet (0.2–0.9 m) tall.

**Notes:** Look for it in meadows and open areas. The lupine is called "bluebonnet" in Texas and is the state flower there.

## CURLY DOCK

**Color:** Starts out green, but is most commonly seen when it is reddish brown. Blooms June to September.

**Size:** 2–4 feet (0.6–1.2 m) tall.

**Notes:** Large areas along roadsides are covered with this introduced plant.

## BLACK-EYED SUSAN

**Color:** Yellow flower with dark brown center. Blooms June to September.

**Size:** 1–2 feet (0.3–0.6 m) tall.

**Notes:** Look alongside roads and dry, open areas of tallgrass and mixed grass prairies. Sometimes large areas will be covered with these flowers.

# Grasses

## NEEDLEGRASS
**Color:** Green, gray-green or purplish.
**Size:** 1–4 feet (0.3–1.2 m) tall.
**Notes:** The stems of this common grassland plant grow in bunches. Their pointed seeds can hurt grazing animals and are one of the reasons for their common names of needle-and-thread and porcupine grass.

## GRAMA GRASS
**Color:** Green with purplish flowers.
**Size:** 6–30 inches (15.2–76.2 cm) tall.
**Notes:** This is one of the most common grasses of the drier grasslands. Look for it in rocky or sandy areas. Blue grama grass is the state grass of Colorado and New Mexico. Sideoats grama is the state grass of Texas.

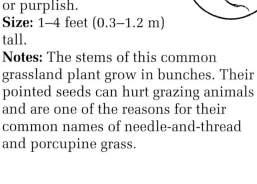

## SACATON
**Color:** Green with some purple.
**Size:** 1–6½ feet (0.3–2.0 m) tall.
**Notes:** This is a common grass of the California Valley and semidesert grasslands and other dry grasslands. Look for it in flat areas that are moist or flooded at least once a year.

## FOXTAIL BARLEY
**Color:** Green, sometimes with a bit of purple mixed in. Light tan when dry.
**Size:** 12–24 inches (30.5–6 cm) tall.
**Notes:** Large areas alongside the road may be covered with foxtail barley. The plants move like swells on the sea as the wind passes over them. If you walk through them, pieces stick in your socks.

## WHEATGRASS
**Color:** Bluish green.
**Size:** From 2–3 feet (0.6–0.9 m) tall.
**Notes:** Grows as large clumps, often sticking up above shorter grasses in open areas. Western wheatgrass is noticeable because of its waxy-looking stems. Bluebunch wheatgrass is the state grass of Montana and Washington.

## LITTLE BLUESTEM
**Color:** Green, turning light reddish brown in the fall.
**Size:** 1–4 feet (0.3–1.2 m) tall.
**Notes:** Look for little bluestem in both dry and moist areas. It is the state grass of Nebraska and a very common grass of the Great Plains.

# Shrubs and Trees

## YUCCA
**Color:** Creamy white flowers. Blooms May to July.
**Size:** 1–3 feet (0.3–0.9 m) tall. Taller when flowering stalks are present.
**Notes:** Plains Indians used the roots of the small soaptree yucca to make a kind of soap. Look for the stiff, sharp leaves of yucca on dry, open hillsides sticking up above the grasses and other plants. Be careful around yuccas … getting stuck on the spiny ends of the leaves hurts a lot! The yucca is the state flower of New Mexico.

## LEADPLANT
**Color:** Purplish flowers and gray-green leaves. Blooms May to August.
**Size:** 1–3 feet (0.3–0.9 m) tall.
**Notes:** Found in dry areas on the prairie.

## RABBITBRUSH
**Color:** Yellow flowers. Blooms July to October.
**Size:** 1–3 feet (0.3–0.9 m) tall.
**Notes:** This is one of the last plants to still be in flower in the fall. Look for it on dry slopes and along roadsides.

## WILLOW
**Color:** Creamy white flowers and green to gray-green leaves.
**Size:** Usually 5–10 feet (1.5–3 m) tall.
**Notes:** Found along streams and other moist areas in all the grasslands. Often grows in thickets.

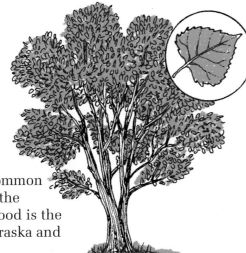

## COTTONWOOD
**Color:** Green leaves, grayish bark.
**Size:** Up to 100 feet (30.5 m) tall.
**Notes:** This is the most common tree along streams in all the grasslands. The cottonwood is the state tree of Kansas, Nebraska and Wyoming.

## CHOKECHERRY
**Color:** Yellowish white flowers from April to May. Dark purple fruits from late July to early August.
**Size:** Up to 20 feet (6.1 m) tall.
**Notes:** Found in ravines and valleys. Plains Indians mixed the fruit with dried meat to make a food called pemmican.

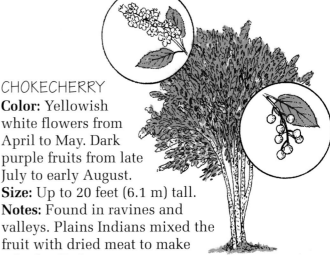

# Animal Tracks

Coyote

The footprints or "tracks" of animals can often be seen in fine dirt or sand. Look also in the mud along the edge of a pond, lake or stream. Tracks may also be found in areas with dry sand or fine, dry dirt, especially alongside the road. How big is each track? Is there more than one kind in an area? Where did you see them? These are the clues that help you figure out the size of the animals, the different kinds that live in an area and where on the grassland they can be found.

Sometimes tracks of different animals actually look very similar. Look at the **bison**, **pronghorn** and **deer** tracks below. These are all related members of a group of animals that have hooves on their feet. So, animal tracks can show not only the different kinds that live in an area, but also those animals that are similar in some way.

Remember that even if you don't see any animals when you visit an area, finding animal tracks is one way of knowing which animals make their homes there.

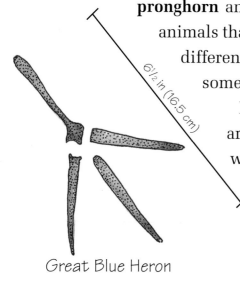
6½ in (16.5 cm)
Great Blue Heron

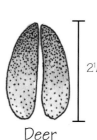
2 in (5 cm)
front
Badger
hind

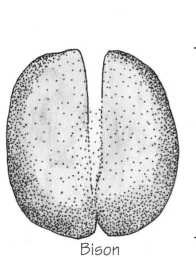
5 in (12.7 cm)
Bison

3 in (7.6 cm)
Pronghorn

2½ in (6.4 cm)
Deer

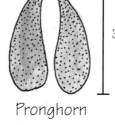
¼ in (0.6 cm)
Deer Mouse

# Glossary

**annuals:** Plants that grow from a seed, make flowers, set seeds and die all within one season or one year.

**biome:** An area that has a specific grouping or community of plants. It may also share climate, topography and soil.

**bunchgrass:** A type of grass that grows in a clump with many stems coming out of a central spot or base.

**draws:** Shallow, canyonlike areas where trees and shrubs may be growing.

**drought:** A period with no rain that can last for many months and sometimes even a year or more.

**grassland:** An area that has more land covered by grasses than by other plants.

**habitat:** An area that contains the special environmental needs of a plant or animal, such as food, cover, water, etc.

**hogwallows:** Low spots or shallow pools from which rainwater does not drain. They can fill up and evaporate several times during a season. Not as deep as vernal pools.

**introduced:** Describes plant or animal that naturally occurs in another area but has been brought to, and is growing in, a different place.

**perennial:** A plant that lives for more than one year.

**plains:** Large open areas of flat or gently rolling countryside.

**prairie:** Name given to some of the grassland areas of North America, especially those in the Great Plains. May also refer to just those areas densely covered with grasses higher than 3 feet (0.9 m) tall.

**prairie potholes:** Depressions or pools, most filled with water year-round, that were formed as glaciers retreated from the northern Great Plains during the last Ice Age, 10,000–12,000 years ago.

**riparian:** An area that has available water year-round, either above or below ground.

**savanna:** A grasslandlike area with scattered trees or woodland cover.

**sod:** A dense, interwoven mat of grass stems and roots just below the surface of the ground.

**vernal pools:** Shallow pools of standing water that form after winter rains and dry up by summer. Rings of wildflowers come and go along the pool's edge as it dries up.

# Resources

The places listed below have prairies or other grasslands open to the public. They may also have hiking trails, a visitor center and a naturalist or ranger to answer questions. Write to them for more information or search for them on the Internet.

## TALLGRASS PRAIRIE

Neal Smith National Wildlife Refuge
P.O. Box 399
Prairie City, IA 50288-0399

Tallgrass Prairie National Preserve
Route 1, Box 14
Strong City, KS 66869

Tallgrass Prairie Preserve
Box 458
Pawhuska, OK 74056

## MIXED-GRASS PRAIRIE

Grasslands National Park
Box 150
Val Marie, Saskatchewan S0N 2T0
Canada

Theodore Roosevelt National Park
P.O. Box 7
Medora, ND 58645

## SHORTGRASS PRAIRIE

Wind Cave National Park
Route 1, Box 190 WCNP
Hot Springs, SD 57747

Cimarron National Grassland
242 Hwy 56 East, Box J
Elkhart, KS 67950

Thunder Basin National Grassland
Douglas Ranger District
2250 E. Richards St
Douglas, WY 82633-8922

## PALOUSE PRAIRIE

National Bison Range
132 Bison Range Road
Moiese, MT 59824

## CALIFORNIA VALLEY GRASSLAND

Great Valley Grassland State Park
31426 Gonzaga Road
Gustine, CA 95322-9737

San Luis National Wildlife Refuge
Complex
P.O. Box 2176
Los Banos, CA 93635

## SEMIDESERT GRASSLAND

Buenos Aires National Wildlife Refuge
P.O. Box 109
Sasabe, AZ 85321

Big Bend National Park
P.O. Box 129
Big Bend National Park, Texas 79834

For a list of all National Grasslands in the United States, write to
National Grasslands Visitor's Center, 708 Main St., P.O. Box 425, Wall, SD 57790.

# List of Common and Scientific Names

If you were in the shortgrass prairie or semidesert grassland of Texas, you might see some bluish purple flowers called "bluebonnets." If you saw the same types of flowers in another grassland, they would probably be called "lupines." **Common names** for plants and animals may be different depending on where you are, who tells you the name, or what you're using to look it up. It can be very confusing. But the **scientific name** of a plant or animal is the same everywhere in the world.

Scientific names have two parts, both of which are underlined or typed in *slanted* letters called "italics." The first part is called the **genus** and is capitalized. The second part is called the **species** and is not capitalized. If a common name refers to more than one species of the same genus, then the name of the genus is followed by "**spp.**"

The following list includes all the plants and animals illustrated in this book.

Agave (*Agave* spp.)
American avocet (*Recurvirostra americana*)
American coot (*Fulica americana*)
American kestrel (*Falco sparverius*)
Arrowleaf balsam root (*Balsamorhiza sagittata*)

Badger (*Taxidea taxus*)
Bandwinged grasshopper (*Trimerotropis pallidipennis*)
Barrel Cactus (*Ferocactus cylindraceus*)
Big bluestem (*Andropogon gerardii*)
Big sagebrush (*Artemisia tridentata*)
Bird's foot violet (*Viola pedata*)
Bison (*Bison bison*) (*Bos bison*)
Bitter cherry (*Prunus emarginata*)
Black-billed magpie (*Pica hudsonia*)
Black-eyed susan (*Rudbeckia hirta*)
Black-necked stilt (*Himantopus mexicanus*)
Black-tailed prairie dog (*Cynomys ludovicianus*)
Blazing star (*Liatris* spp.)
Blue grama (*Bouteloua gracilis*)
Bluebunch wheatgrass (*Pseudoroegneria spicata*)
Bluegill (*Lepomis macrochirus*)
Bobolink (*Dolichonyx oryzivorus*)
Box turtle (*Terrapene* spp.)
Buffalo bunchgrass (*Festuca scabrella*)
Buffalo grass (*Bouteloua dactyloides*)

Bullfrog (*Rana catesbeiana*)
Bullsnake (*Pituophis melanoleucus*)
Bur oak (*Quercus macrocarpa*)
Burrograss (*Scleropogon brevifolius*)
Burrowing owl (*Athene cunicularia*)
Burying beetle (*Nicrophorus* spp.)
Bush muhly (*Muhlenbergia porteri*)
Butterfly milkweed (*Asclepias tuberosa*)

Cabbage white (*Artogeia rapae*)
California ground squirrel (*Spermophilus beecheyi*)
California poppy (*Eschscholzia californica*)
Camas (*Quamasia quamash*)
Canada wild rye (*Elymus canadensis*)
Catclaw (*Acacia gregggii*)
Cheatgrass (*Bromus tectorum*)
Chokecherry (*Prunus virginiana*)
Coachwhip (*Maticophis flagellum*)
Collared lizard (*Chrotaphytus collaris*)
Common sunflower (*Helianthus annuus*)
Compass plant (*Silphium laciniatum*)
Cottontail (*Sylvilagus* spp.)
Cottonwood (*Populus* spp.)
Coyote (*Canis latrans*)
Creeping wild rye (*Elymus triticoides*)
Curly dock (*Rumex crispus*)

Deer mouse (*Peromyscus maniculatus*)
Devil's claw (*Proboscidea altheaefolia*)
Dickcissel (*Spiza americana*)

Douglas fir (*Pseudotsuga menziesii*)
Downingia Dragonfly (*Downingia* spp.)
Dragonfly (various species)
Dung beetle (*Canthon* spp.)

Eastern kingbird (*Tyrannus tyrannus*)
Egret (*Family Ardeidae*)
Elderberry (*Sambucus* spp.)
Elk (*Cerus elaphus*)
Evening primrose (*Oenothera* spp.)

Fiddleneck (*Amsinckia retrorsa*)
Fire ant/Desert fire ant (*Solenopsis xyloni*)
Foxtail barley (*Hordeum jubatum*)
Fritillary butterfly (different genera)

Garter snake (*Thamnophis* spp.)
Giant swallowtail (*Papilio cresphontes*)
Golden eagle (*Aquila chrysaetos*)
Goldenrod (*Solidago* spp.)
Goldfields (*Lasthenia californica*)
Gopher snake (*Pituophis melanoceucus*)
Grasshopper sparrow (*Ammodramus savannarum*)
Gray partridge (*Perdix perdix*)
Gray-headed coneflower (*Ratibida pinnata*)
Great blue heron (*Ardea herodias*)
Great Plains pocket gopher (*Geomys bursarius*)
Greater roadrunner (*Geococcyx californianus*)

Harvester ant (*Pogonomyrmex* spp.)
Hilltop daisy (*Monolopia lanceolata*)
Horned lark (*Eremophila alpestris*)
Horned lizard (*Phrynosoma* spp.)
Horselubber grasshopper (*Taeniopoda eques*)

Idaho fescue (*Festuca idahoensis*)
Indian grass (*Sorghastrum nutans*)
Iodine bush (*Allenrolfea occidentalis*)

Jackrabbit (*Lepus* spp.)
Javelina (*Tayassu tajacu*)
Junegrass (*Koeleria* spp.)

Kangaroo rat (*Dipodomys* spp.)
Killdeer (*Charadrius vociferus*)
Killifish (*Fundulus zebrinus*)

Ladybug (*Coccinella* spp.)
Largemouth bass (*Micropterus salmoides*)
Lark bunting (*Calamospiza melanocorys*)
Leadplant (*Amorpha canescens*)
Lechuguilla (*Agave lecheguilla*)
Lehmann lovegrass (*Eragrostis lehmanniana*)
Leopard frog (*Rana* spp.)
Little bluestem (*Schizachyrum scopariom*)
Living rock cactus (*Ariocarpus fissuratus*)
Loggerhead shrike (*Lanius ludovicianus*)
Lubber grasshopper (*Brachystola magna*)
Lupine (*Lupinus* spp.)

Massasauga (*Sistrurus catenatus*)
Meadow vole *(Microtus pennsylvanicus)*
Meadowfoam (*Limnanthes* spp.*)*
Meadowlark (*Sturnella* spp.*)*
Mesquite (*Prosopis glandulosa*)
Monarch (*Danaus plexippus*)
Mountain bluebird (*Sialia currucoides*)
Mourning dove (*Zenaida macroura*)
Mule deer (*Odocoileus hemionus*)

Needlegrass (*Stipa* spp.)
Northern harrier (*Circus cyaneus*)

Ornate tiger moth (*Apantesis ornata*)
Owl's clover (*Castilleja* spp.)

Pacific tree frog (*Hyla regilla*)
Paintbrush (*Castilleja* spp.)
Painted lady butterfly (*Vanessa cardui*)

Painted turtle (*Chrysemys picta*)
Pale purple coneflower (*Echinacea pallida*)
Palo verde (*Cercidium* spp.)
Pasqueflower (*Pulsatilla patens*)
Pinacate beetle or Stink beetle (*Eleodes* spp.)
Pocket gopher (*Thomomys* spp.)
Ponderosa pine (*Pinus ponderosa*)
Prairie coneflower (*Ratibida columnifera*)
Prairie dropseed (*Sporobolus heterolepis*)
Prairie falcon (*Falco mexicanus*)
Prairie vole (*Microtus ochrogaster*)
Prickly pear (*Opuntia* spp.)
Prickly poppy (*Argemone polyanthemos*)
Pronghorn (*Antilocapra americana*)
Purple needlegrass (*Stipa pulchra*)
Purple prickly pear (*Opuntia santa-rita*)

Rabbitbrush (*Chrysothamnus nauseosus*)
Rattlesnake (*Crotalus* spp.)
Rattesnake master (*Eryngium yuccifolium*)
Red-tailed hawk (*Buteo jamaicensis*)
Red-winged blackbird (*Agelaius phoeniceus*)
Ring-necked pheasant (*Phasianus colchicus*)
Rocky Mountain bee plant (*Cleome serrulata*)

Sacaton (*Sporobolus* spp.)
Saltgrass (*Distichlis spicata*)
Sandhill crane (*Grus canadensis*)
Scaled quail (*Callipepla squamata*)
Scarlet globemallow (*Sphaeralcea coccinea*)
Sego lily (*Calochortus gunnisonii*)
Serviceberry (*Amelanchier* spp.)
Sharp-tailed grouse (*Tympanuchus phasianellus*)
Shooting star (*Dodocatheon clevelandia*)
Showy milkweed (*Asclepias speciosa*)
Side-oats grama (*Bouteloua curtipendula*)
Small soapweed (*Yucca glauca*)
Smooth sumac (*Rhus glabra*)
Snakeweed (*Gutierrezia sarothrae*)
Snowberry (*Symphoricarpos occidentalis*)
Soaptree yucca (*Yucca elata*)
Soft chess (*Bromus mollis*)
Sotol (*Dasylirion wheeleri*)

Spotted frog (*Rana pretiosa*)
Striped skunk (*Mephitis mephitis*)
Sulfur butterfly (*Colias* spp.)
Swainson's hawk (*Buteo swainsoni*)
Swift fox (*Vulpes velox*)
Switchgrass (*Panicum virgatum*)

Tarantula (*Aphonopelma chalcodes*)
Thirteen-lined ground squirrel (*Spermophilus tridecemlineatus*)
Thistle/Star thistle (*Centaurea solstitialis*)
Tidy-tips (*Layia* spp.)
Tiger salamander (*Ambystoma tigrinum*)
Tiger swallowtail (*Papillo* spp.)
Tobosa (*Pleuraphis mutica*)
Tule (*Scirpus acutus*)
Tule elk (*Cervus elaphus*)
Turkey vulture (*Cathartes aura*)

Upland sandpiper (*Bartramia longicauda*)

Valley oak (*Quercus lobata*)
Vermilion flycatcher (*Pyrocephalus rubinus*)
Vervain (*Verbena* spp.)

Wait-a-minute bush (*Mimosa biuncifera*)
Walleye (*Stizostedion vitreum*)
Western toad (*Bufo boreas)*
Western wheatgrass (*Pascopyrum smithii*)
Whiptail lizard (*Cnemidophorus* spp.)
White-tailed kite (*Elanus leucurus)*
White thorn (*Acacia constricta*)
White-tailed deer (*Odocoileus virginianus*)
Wild oats (*Avena fatua*)
Wild plum (*Prunus americana*)
Wild rose (*Rosa* spp.)
Willow (*Salix* spp.)
Windscorpion (Order Solpugida)
Woodhouse's toad (*Bufo woodhousei*)

Yarrow (*Achillea* spp.)
Yellow sweet clover (*Melilotus officinalis*)
Yucca (*Yucca* spp.)
Yucca moth (*Tegeticula yuccasella)*

# Index

bird's foot violets